160 Characters or Less

How to Increase Customer Loyalty, Drive Sales and WIN with Text Message Marketing

By Judd Wheeler

Edited by Vickie Dawkins-Kersey

ISBN-10: 1502853795

ISBN-13: 978-0-1502853790

Library of Congress Control Number: 2014916682

Copyright © 2014 Judd Wheeler

All rights reserved, including the right of reproduction in whole or in part in any form, electronic, mechanical, photocopying, recording or otherwise without written permission.

While every precaution has been taken in the preparation of this book, the publisher and author assume no responsibility for errors or omissions, or for damages resulting from the use of the information contained herein.

*This book is dedicated to
my adorable daughter,
Reese.
I love you dearly.*

*And to my father, Jack Wheeler, who
inspired me, brought technology
into my life and loved me.*

Special thanks to Vickie for editing my spaghetti writing style; Matt Galloway, Jeff Rhoton, my fifth grade teacher, Ms. Black (who always told me I should write for a living); and of course, Mom who makes all things possible.

Table of Contents

Contents

Introduction 6
Text Message Marketing Is Personalized Engagement 9
Outbound Versus Inbound Marketing 12
The Text Message Lexicon 14
Short Codes Versus Long Codes 19
SMS Gateway Versus SMS Marketing Platform 21
Choosing the Right SMS Marketing Platform 22
Choosing a Keyword 25
How to Get Customers and Potential Customers to Sign Up 27
Auto Reply When Signing Up 29
How to Keep Your Text-based Subscribers 31
Personalization 34
How Often Should You Text? 36
Make Your SMS Marketing More Viral 37
Different Ways to Use SMS 39
Best Practices 47
Guidelines from the Mobile Marketing Association (MMA) 53
Telephone Consumer Protection Act – "TCPA" (the other text messaging rules) 59
Track Your SMS Marketing Campaigns 61

Return on Investment (ROI) 64

The Significance of the Unsubscribe 65

Examples of Successful (and Not So Successful) SMS Campaigns........68

#Fail 74

Text Versus Email 76

Next-Gen Messaging Apps: Will it Kill SMS Marketing? 79

Summary 81

Epilogue 84

About the Author 88

Introduction

Over the past 20 years, I've watched how businesses utilize technology for marketing. For eight years, I've focused primarily on mobile technologies, spending most of my time talking to professionals in the mobile world, and more importantly, the businesses they serve. I've spoken with big businesses, small businesses and their customers. I've traveled the world speaking at conferences and interviewing people in restaurants, stores and hotel lobbies about mobile technology. No one was off-limits when it came to understanding how businesses and customers could now connect through their mobile devices.

Keeping up with the latest research is daunting to say the least; evolutionary change is inevitable when it comes to technology. But what I've discovered in a nutshell is that mobile technology is an effective and cost-efficient means of marketing. The problem is, businesses either aren't using it at all or not exploiting the full measure of mobile marketing advantages. It's a bit discouraging. The amount of time we spend with our mobile phones today dwarfs our time spent with any other media channel and often the people in our lives. Don't believe me? Just take a look around the mall, your favorite restaurant, the folks standing in line at the grocery store or dry cleaners. How many people do you see with their heads down, fingers moving, faces illuminated by the light of a device that's become an extension of their lives?

Whether they're texting, playing games, posting photos on Facebook, or figuring out how to manipulate Twitter's 140 character limit, they are using their cell phones. At any moment around the world, people on foot are walking into traffic, narrowly escaping brushes with death by a two-ton automobile. Teens text during sex. Adults walk obliviously into fountains. We now regularly miss our favorite television shows and their financially supported commercials because we play Words with Friends or browse our tablets for the latest Brangelina gossip.

All of this because the power of mobile technology now commands our full attention.

After working with numerous businesses and marketers, I've discovered a great disconnect between what they believe mobile is and can do, and what mobile really is and can do. There are myths and misconceptions about the entire industry. There is a fear of making costly or embarrassing mistakes, and a general lack of understanding the rules and regulations.

So, here we are with the first in a series of mobile marketing books beginning with this one: *160 Characters or Less: How to Increase Loyalty, Drive Sales and WIN with Text Message Marketing.* I've chosen to tackle this topic first for a couple of reasons. First, I believe text message marketing is one of today's most cost-effective marketing tactics. If done correctly, the return on investment can be enormous. Second, there are probably more rules and regulations involved with text message marketing in the U.S. than other forms of mobile marketing; therefore, businesses should have a full grasp of these before launching their campaigns. Third, marketers simply cannot trust every text message marketing platform out there and need to know what to watch out for.

While this book is primarily focused on business-to-consumer (B2C) marketing, business-to-business (B2B) marketers can also utilize text message marketing. Leveraging a multi-channel approach that includes text message marketing can deliver impressive results no matter who your audience may be.

Text Message Marketing Is Personalized Engagement

For years, businesses have searched for ways to ingratiate their brand, products or services into the personal lives of their customers, and to create touch points wherever those customers are. Billions of dollars are spent every year on print advertising, billboards, radio, television, and the Internet. Marketers practically shout at the corner of every street in the hope a potential customer walks or drives by, but never knowing for certain if their message is heard—or more importantly—acted upon. Believe it or not, the first text message was sent out more than 20 years ago, its originator unaware how this simple message system would forever change the way we personalize and target customers.

As businesses attempt to make more money while spending less, text marketing may be better suited than other forms of advertising to achieve this goal. The figure below presents an average cost per thousand (CPM) numbers for a few different media types.

Media Types	Average CPM
Billboard – 30-Sheet Poster*	$2.05
Radio Ad – During Prime Drive Time*	$8.61
Magazine – One page with 4 colors*	$9.35
Text Message Marketing	*$10.00*
Television Commercial – 30 seconds on a prime-time network*	$17.78
Newspaper – 1/3 page in black & White*	$22.95

*According to OAAA

At first glance it would appear that billboards, radio spots and magazines present better value than text message marketing;

however, the calculations of CPM can be misleading. CPM is based on how much advertising costs to reach 1,000 people.

Let's look at billboards. The value of billboards is calculated by multiplying the daily traffic volume by the number of days the billboard will be posted, divided by 1,000, divided by the cost of the monthly rent. Magazines and newspapers, on the other hand, are calculated by the cost of the ad, divided by the circulation, times 1,000. But neither of these calculations— billboard or magazines and newspapers— take into account how many drivers or newspaper subscribers actually *viewed* the ad. Since the dawn of smartphones, most people today are looking at their phones while driving. Forget the billboard; we just hope the drivers see us ahead of them. Forget actually *watching* the commercials. Unless it's the Super Bowl, most people are looking at their mobile devices, not your three-million-dollar-plus spot.

Here's where personalized engagement comes into play. Traditional media, as calculated above, can't provide the opportunity for direct, individual, two-way communication with the consumer. But text messaging, also known as SMS, can. The direct, individual nature of text messaging makes it innately personal, even intimate. Our phones are so personal, in fact, that studies show the number one item husbands and wives refuse to share is their mobile phone.

Text message marketing is also an easy, quick form of communication. Consider the ubiquitous magazine ad. You first need to develop a slam-dunk concept. Your writer and designer have to make that concept come alive through compelling words and head-turning design. Then comes the multiple approval processes. Changes are made. Then changes to the changes are made. Finally, someone (usually the client or company executive) sprinkles their final blessing on your work of art and it's off to the magazine, where marketers wait months to finally see their creation in print. With text marketing, you hone your mail list (more on that later), craft the message, and send the text to the hundreds or thousands of people who have asked to receive your marketing message. People who may be followers, customers or potential customers. People who want to hear from you. There are no big production time and cost expenses for you and the process happens practically immediately. Let's say you're a small business and experiencing a slow day. What can attract your customers to your doorstep right away? A limited time offer, of course. Simply, write up that offer and text it. No fuss, no muss, no waiting months for results.

How many people still read the newspaper? Most newspapers today are clinging to life support. That's because nearly 85% of Americans own a cell phone and more than 90% carry their phone everywhere they go, including the bathroom. According to a November 2012 Pew Report, 81% use SMS (97% of 18-29 year-olds and 92% of 30-49 year olds). These numbers blow away every other form of marketing or advertising available today.

Americans prefer coupons via text. In a study conducted by the UK Direct Marketing Association (DMA), one-third of Americans would rather receive offers via text. Receiving offers by way of email came in at 21%. Approximately 11% preferred mobile apps. In addition, 63% of marketers cite "immediacy" as the number one benefit of using SMS campaigns, followed by high open rates and low cost. You can see why I believe consumer attitudes are not only changing but evolving with technology.

While I get excited about the potential for marketers using text marketing, I can also understand why it isn't viewed as sexy. At the outset, businesses struggle to find any glamour in text so they often think it's not worthy of their time and effort. In my experience, nothing could be further from the truth. In 2011, Ford conducted a text campaign that resulted in a 15.4% increase in consumer awareness. Ford asked readers of the ad to text FORD to a short code for more information about purchasing a new vehicle. This led to a few more prompts that provided the local dealers with information to contact the interested buyer. Try getting those results spending the same amount of money on any other marketing platform.

The way we shop, the way we live our lives are now mobile.

Outbound Versus Inbound Marketing

With advertising targets on our foreheads, we consumers have been subjected to unwanted outbound marketing for years. We regularly check our mailboxes only to find them stuffed with junk mail. We eagerly wait for the TV commercials to end so we can find out who did it on our favorite television shows. We jump between radio stations on our way to work to avoid the radio spot. Poor marketers. They've had to rely on limited forms of advertising to sell us their products and services, and those forms of advertising are no longer working.

Why are they not working? The Internet. The Internet has empowered consumers with alternative ways to find, buy and research brands and products. The Internet has opened a two-way dialogue that has expanded with social media. The Internet has reduced the cost per lead as marketers, and given us new opportunities to build relationships with our customers. The Internet has paved the road for inbound marketing.

Outbound marketing offers consumers products and services whether or not they want or need them. This is interruptive marketing and includes television, print ads, direct mailers, radio, robo calls and more. Outbound marketing can be expensive and is rarely timely, although it can benefit larger companies or recognized brands that need to get a product or service noticed at the national level.

Inbound marketing, on the other hand, presents immeasurable opportunities to small businesses. If you provide quality content, the cost is low enough for tactics like blogging, social media, search engine optimization, pay-per-click and, yes, text message marketing, to compete with the "big boys" and succeed. Inbound marketing is all about turning strangers into customers by generating demand for your products and services that begins with building trust with your audience.

Some marketers may put social media and text message marketing in the outbound marketing category. And, sometimes, they would be correct. For example, there are companies that use text message marketing exclusively to push deals and offers. The problem is they don't allow for communication. This is homogenous to getting an email from "do-not-reply@xyz.com." Everyone receives the same offer, the same deal, and no one is made to feel special.

Text message marketing, at its core, is about more than shot-gunned deals and offers. Why? Your offers are personalized and your deals are based on targeted demographics. Texting customer surveys and polls convert the marketing channel from outbound to inbound. The opportunity for two-way communication with your customers can make the outbound-to-inbound switch happen in your business.

Getting the right products and services into the hands of the people who want them, who asked for them, who are more inclined to purchase them, is what inbound marketing is all about. However, text message marketing can also galvanize the impulse buy that outbound marketing is good for. Sometimes, a potential customer doesn't even know they need something until you tell them they do, or simply let them know you have it. Text message marketing can combine the best of both worlds.

The Text Message Lexicon

Before diving into the meat of text message marketing, let's examine some of the basic terms you'll encounter in this electronic marketing world. If you are familiar with text message marketing, you can probably skip to the next chapter.

SMS Marketing = Text Message Marketing

CTIA is the wireless association that makes all the rules about text message marketing and enforces them through random audits. CTIA used to stand for Cellular Telecommunications Industry Association in 2000, then became the Cellular Telecommunications and Internet Association in 2004. These are the guys that repealed the IRS property rule on mobile devices and help states model legislation that would make manual texting while driving illegal.

TCPA stands for Telephone Consumer Protection Act. This is the law that protects us from getting unwanted robo calls from telemarketers

Wireless Carrier is the group you pay way too much money for every month to have mobile phone service

Major Carriers are companies like AT&T, Verizon, Sprint, and T-Mobile

Minor Carriers are companies like Cellular One, Cricket, Mosiac, Hawkeye, and Alaska Communication Systems

Short Codes are common 5- or 6-digit numbers assigned and administered by the U.S. Common short Code Administrator (CSCA). Short codes do not work across the borders of different countries. Short codes can be leased for three to 12 months for $500 per month for a random code, and $1,000 for a vanity short code. A vanity short code is a specific set of numbers that you request.

Long Codes are 10-digit phone numbers like the phone numbers we're used to seeing. These are now "virtual numbers" that support SMS and other functions like real phones. These codes can work across borders, and many countries outside the U.S. use them since smaller, less developed countries don't have the current infrastructure to handle their own short codes.

Private Short Code is a short code that is leased by one company and only used by that company. The company that leases the short code has unlimited keywords that can be used to communicate with consumers.

Shared Short Code is a short code that is shared across multiple businesses. Keywords are generally limited by the plan and cannot be duplicated. For example, if Domino's Pizza and Papa John's Pizza were using the same messaging service and sharing the same short code, only one of the companies could use the keyword PIZZA. The other company would have to choose something else.

SMTP (Simple Mail Transfer Protocol) is an Internet standard for electronic mail transmission.

SMPP (Short Message Peer-to-Peer) is an open industry standard protocol used by the telecommunications industry for quickly delivering SMS messages.

A **Keyword** is a word or name used to distinguish a targeted message within a Short Code Service. Let's look at the following:

Text REDCROSS to 90999 to donate $10

REDCROSS is the keyword and 90999 is the short code. Another way to look at it is 90999 is the domain name like www.themobilists.com and REDCROSS is the page you want to go to.

Click-to-Call is a phone number that you receive through a text, email, or on a web page that you can click and the phone automatically dials the number

Msg&Data Rates May Apply is standard text at the bottom of most text message campaigns that means standard message rates and data charges from your carrier apply when sending and/or receiving texts

Double Opt-In is the process of confirming a mobile subscriber's desire to join a mobile program by requesting the subscriber to opt-in twice.

Split Testing is a simple randomized experiment with text copy variants. For example, A/B testing would include two variants. Let's say you have a database of 2,000 customers. You would send 1,000 people a message that reads, "Offer ends this Saturday! Text A1 to receive your coupon." Another 1,000 people would receive "Offer ends soon! Text B1 to receive your coupon." You can then determine how many people responded to A1 versus B1 to assess which message was the most effective.

Application Programming Interface (API), in computer language, specifies how software components interact with each other. For example, how a website interacts with a database, or an app uses graphical user interface components that are built into the operating system (like iOS or Android) on a smartphone.

Major Messaging Types:
Short Message Service (SMS) is a text messaging service of mobile phones that is limited to 160 characters and only contains plain text (no images, video, etc.). This is what we will focus on in this book. SMS messages are either considered mobile originated (MO) or mobile terminated (MT). MO messages are sent from a mobile phone. MT messages are sent to a mobile phone from a messaging platform, which is generally sent from a computer (or server) by an established service provider that has special bulk rates with the wireless carriers (like AT&T, T-Mobile, etc.).

Multimedia Messaging Service (MMS) is the standard system to send messages that include content like pictures and video, or long messages in a single message. It is possible to deliver files of up to 1MB or higher depending on the carrier file size restrictions. This is why you see your pictures and video having to compress before sending on smartphones.

Push Notifications are delivered via a mobile app on a smartphone and is a service built into the device. These are typically free messages. Mobile service providers have platforms that send high volumes of these messages to subscribers for a fee.

Over-The-Top Messaging (OTT) is a way to send messages like MMS through mobile apps developed by third parties (not carriers) which are downloaded by consumers to their devices. The only cost associated with these messages is the data cost of the consumer's plan. Examples of OTT are Apple's iMessage, WhatsApp and BlackBerry's BMM messenger.

Premium SMS was launched in 2004 when a customer's carrier would charge for messages received by cell phone. Text messages might be in the form of insider information about celebrities, shows, sports figures, etc. Customers pay to receive these messages and the carriers bill them for each. But premium SMS services come at a high cost to both customers and carriers with an estimated $2 billion a year in fraudulent charges. Not only are these charges taxing to consumers who are victimized but to carriers who have to recoup the revenue loss by raising monthly cell phone rates. In late 2013, major carriers like AT&T, Sprint, T-Mobile and Verzion dropped most premium SMS billing. The one premium service they will continue to support is charitable giving and political donations.

New and more effective billing solutions, such as PayPhone and BilltoMobil, have launched since the advent of premium SMS.

Short Codes Versus Long Codes

Two different codes can be used to send text messages to your customers. Long codes are 10-digit numbers like what we're used to seeing when you type in or enter a phone number to call someone. Short codes are 5- or 6-digit numbers like 55678.

Long Codes

Generally, long code per-message fees are higher than short codes, however, the set-up and monthly costs make them more affordable. A customer opt-in process is not required due to the lack of a vetting process to lease a short code, which means long code messages can also be used for spamming. This is obviously a big issue. A major drawback is that long codes are hard to remember. There is also a speed limit to the number of messages that can be sent at one time. The use of long codes makes it impossible for businesses to provide free texting for their subscribers, so the text message cost falls on the subscribers when they receive or send texts.

There are a few places where I see a big advantage using long codes. The first place is during development of an app or testing a campaign. The setup is very quick and the costs are generally much less when sending a limited number of messages. The second is any app utilizing text messages could benefit from long code costs. The third place would be internal business communications.

Short Codes

For many businesses, short codes can be cost-prohibitive with set monthly costs on top of the per message cost. Short codes have to be individually activated for each country and approved by the carrier. While it can be a long and costly process to own your own short code, you can lease or share short codes from companies like Tatango, HipCricket or imobilize media and pay only monthly costs.

Shared short codes advantages include time-to-market and cost. However, the downside can be brand confusion. There really isn't much brand value in using a shared short code. In many cases, there are competing businesses using the same short code that you are.

Dedicated short codes are brand-friendly and you can market the heck out of it, embedding it into your customers' or potential customers' brain. Dedicated short codes can create a better user experience by not having to compete for keywords. When using a shared short code, you're never going to get the keyword PIZZA. However, you can if you have a dedicated short code. Unfortunately, there is the cost ($15,000-$30,000 per year) and time-to-market drawbacks that make it less desirable. You will have to make the call as to the right direction for your campaign.

Vanity short codes are a string of 5-6 digits that are purposely selected by a brand because they're either easy to remember or have a special meaning specific to the brand. Vanity short codes cost about $1,000 per month.

Random short codes are just that—a short code that is randomly selected by The Common Short Code Administration when you register. This means you must take whatever number they give you. The cost of a random short code is about $500 per month.

The vetting process to own a dedicated short code can take weeks or even months, but the vetting time makes short codes less susceptible to spam. Mobile Marketing Association (MMA), FCC and carriers have put rules in place to protect consumers. Failure to comply can cost money and can get you blacklisted. These rules are addressed more in depth later on in the book. Short codes allow businesses to make the texts they send and receive free to the customer.

SMS Gateway Versus SMS Marketing Platform

There's been much discussion about whether brands should use a SMS gateway (also known as SMS aggregator), like Twilio, or a SMS marketing platform like imobilize media, HipCricket or Tatango. SMS gateways give software developers the ability to write a piece of code to send and receive SMS messages. SMS marketing platforms provide non-developers, such as business owners and marketers, the ability to send and receive text messages; pre-built features, such as contests, polls and autoresponders; and reporting and support to manage text messaging marketing campaigns.

In the early days of the gateway platform Twilio, this utilized 10-digit numbers to send and receive text messages, which means we all now have access to short codes to send messages, using this service.

Here's the breakdown as I see it. Twilio is great for early-stage development projects and internal business communications. If you have a sound software development group that can build out a platform to send and/or receive SMS messages using APIs (application programming interfaces), then SMS gateways can be a great way for you to save some money. However, if your goal is to run successful marketing campaigns, shorten the timeline without development, and adhere to the rules and regulations to avoid lawsuits, I'd strongly suggest SMS marketing platforms. Good SMS marketing platforms can help you navigate through the legalities and best practices.

So, how do you choose the right one?

Choosing the Right SMS Marketing Platform

The marriage of your marketing team and SMS marketing platform provider is crucial to the success of any text marketing campaign. If you choose the wrong company, the campaign could become very costly. You could lose customers, lose sales or even worse, end up in a lawsuit. So how do you select the right SMS marketing platform?

Like any marketing service, price is only a part of the decision. Getting a good deal on a used Ford F-150 truck without an engine doesn't do you any good when you need a semi to deliver all your packages across the nation.

Look at how SMS marketing platforms are sending text messages. SMTP is used for sending emails, which can also be used to send texts. The pitfall here is that many carriers won't accept mass texts through this method and you could be exposed to spam regulations resulting in a bad legal situation. SMPP is the route you want to go here, but make sure the platforms you are considering support all the major carriers.

Demo before buying. Many platforms tout a plethora of features. Only by test-driving the platform can you see if they actually work correctly and determine how easy or hard the setup is. The key here: Look for platforms that are intuitive and easy to use.

Set goals. Good marketing strategies should contain goals. Determine any features needed that will reach these goals and make sure that the platform easily can do them.

Reporting. Reporting. Reporting. Ensure you have a dedicated dashboard to track your campaigns. Metrics are critical to the success of your text messaging campaigns. How do you determine or quantify the campaigns that worked best? How will you deploy split testing? Can you export the reports? You need to know your churn rate (the measure of the number of people leaving you), how many new subscribers you've gained, how many people have unsubscribed (and when), and be able to segment and break down the demographics of your campaigns.

Contacts. You must own your contacts. I cannot stress this enough. If you leave the platform, can you take the contact database with you? If you ever become displeased with the service or outgrow their capabilities, you need the ability to download the contact list to a CSV or XML file. After all, you've spent time and money building your database, your customer list. Don't leave without it.

Scheduling and time-based event handling. The platform you choose should have a comprehensive scheduling component so you can set up time parameters connected to your messages. Can the system work automatically based on your preferences? For example, can texts be automatically sent to your customers the week of their birthday?

Speed. How fast will messages be sent?

Social. Omni-channel or multichannel is all the rage with its seamless and targeted approach focused on the consumer experience through all marketing channels. Does the platform have the ability to post to Twitter and Facebook and send the message to your SMS database all at once?

Support. Does the platform have a contact support to help you with your campaign? How quickly do they respond to client calls? Will they help you set up your website and/or Facebook to handle subscriptions to your text message campaign online?

Continuous improvement. When was the last time the platform added new features? What were the features? What does the platform's future roadmap look like? You never want to fall behind your competition, so ask so you can ensure you stay out in front.

Mobile marketing experts. These are experts to help you grow your database. They understand that your marketing goals are not all about the technology; they're about connecting with people. When choosing a mobile marketing expert to work with, ensure they have a good understanding of your big- picture marketing strategy. They should know how to run a pilot with strict A/B/C testing to measure return on investment (ROI). I recommend choosing a platform company that provides an account executive who takes the time to talk through my campaigns and to brainstorm the best way to reach targeted audiences and provide the right content.

Best practices. Later on, I will address the legal aspects and best practices of SMS marketing. The company you chose to work with should know the Mobile Marketing Association's best practices, carrier guidelines and FCC regulations like the back of their hand and adhere to all of them. If they don't, walk away.

Auto-culling. The platform you choose should be able to delete any numbers that bounce back. In other words, any mobile phone numbers that are kicked back to the system as undeliverable because the number is no longer in service should be automatically removed from your subscriber database and tracked in a report to which you have access.

Security. Offers database back-ups and redundancy.

Choosing a Keyword

When planning your text marketing campaign, one of the most important strategies you should consider is the selection of a keyword. Here are a few tips to help you through the process.

One: Keep it simple

Your chosen keyword must be a word the customer recognizes and associates with your brand and/or promotion. Don't get too fancy or creative. Don't make the keyword so long that customers are discouraged entering it simply because of its length. Simplicity makes the keyword easy to remember. Your potential customers generally have a short time to see the keyword before they move on to the next thing.

Two: Don't use special characters

Think about the steps one must take to locate and enter a special character on a mobile device. Make your keyword ridiculously easy for the customer to remember and enter. Unfortunately, auto-correct or predictive text features on smartphones can sabotage keywords with special characters, replacing them with words that have nothing to do with your promotion or brand. The fact is, most people don't give a second thought to what they text in return. This is evident from all the "Damn you auto correct" sites that give us so much enjoyment.

Three: One word is better than two (or more)

Try your best to use one word as the keyword. The longer the keyword the more confusing it is and the less likely customers will take the time to use it.

Four: Watch your spelling

I know we live in a world where cute and different spellings can help companies stand out. However, at the end of the day, people are likely to enter the correct spelling of a word rather than the unique way you spell it. Ultimately, unique spellings are a headache for everyone and may lead your customers to a competitor if you're sharing a short code. Again, visit "Damn you auto correct" websites.

How to Get Customers and Potential Customers to Sign Up

Text message marketing comes with a double edge sword. Part of the beauty of text marketing is that it is permission-based. Only people who want your messaging are those who get your marketing message. This certainly increases the effectiveness and, thus, the ROI. Unfortunately, the flip side is that your message only goes out to those customers alone. If your database isn't populated, you're losing out. So the question I am asked more than any other on the SMS marketing topic is, "How do I grow my database?"

Growing your customer SMS database doesn't have to be a complex or elaborate process. For example, I shopped at a clothing store recently where I observed a sign in the dressing room. The sign communicated a clear value statement, "Sign up today by texting Savings to 55678 for $5 off your next purchase." And I did. That little 8.5x 11 piece of paper motivated me to take advantage of the offer and make a purchase I might not have otherwise made. The promotion posted in the dressing room also encouraged me to opt-in to receive the store's marketing promotions going forward.

Seattle Sun Tan, a 35-location Seattle tanning salon chain, didn't have an existing mobile phone number database when it launched its first text messaging campaign. Seattle Sun Tan's offer was $20 off an existing customer's next purchase if that customer joined its mobile VIP club. The company grew 4,774 subscribers in one month and generated almost $200,000 in new revenue. How did Seattle Sun Tan do it? The company used its pre-existing email database of 80,000-plus customers, in-store marketing at 35 locations, and social media channels with a direct reach to 37,000-plus customers to advertise the launch of a new SMS campaign. Approximately 57% of recipients redeemed the text message offer and those who did, spent 500% more on average than customers who didn't receive the offer.

Following are some other SMS growth strategies to consider:

1. Leverage your website. Enable customers and potential customers the ability to sign up for text messaging coupons, contests, specials and discounts. Take advantage of search engine marketing (for example, Google AdWords) to direct customers to a special landing page to sign up
2. Encourage your customers to share the offer. If you communicate a compelling offer and invite the customer to share it with their friends and family, most likely they will
3. Host a contest. Customers like to take a chance to win a great prize. Texting makes it easy to enter a contest as opposed to spending a valuable five minutes filling out paperwork and wondering if the contest is really worth the time spent doing so. How does a company get a million and a half people to participate in a contest for five weeks? McDonalds launched a Merry Christmas in the Restaurant sweepstakes in its Italian locations. Customers entered the competition while in the restaurant for the chance to win instant prizes. McDonalds printed short codes on food packaging with prizes ranging from free mobile content to free burgers. The result, more than 1.5 million participants in five weeks. That represented a 25% response rate
4. Ensure that all email campaigns contain a link to subscribe to your texting campaign

5. Add a text call-to-action on all TV, radio, print and outdoor ads. Aveeno, a skin and hair care provider in the U.S., included calls to action on all its printed magazine ads, as it should. This particular call to action used a text message number that offered customers a free skin or hair care sample with an opportunity to opt-in to receive coupons and additional offers. This offer allowed Aveeno to continue to campaign to the customers who opted-in and, thus, grow its database
6. Advertise on other websites, especially to promote events and trade shows
7. Print the incentive, code and keyword at the bottom of your point-of-sale receipts

A new study from Mintel drives these points home. Millennials are about twice as likely as Baby Boomers to share cell phone numbers with marketers (30% vs. 14%). What's even more interesting for SMS marketers is the fact that 51% of Millennials said they would be swayed by an incentive offer to do so, whereas for Baby Boomers, only 25% could be swayed by these same types of incentives.

Incentives are the most important part of compelling customers or potential customers to share their number with you.

Auto Reply When Signing Up

The auto reply is a special message that is automatically sent to a customer when they opt-in for your text marketing. It's important to keep your auto reply message clear and concise so there is no confusion by the recipient.

Here are a few components that every good auto reply message should contain.

Confirm Subscription
Confirm that the customer has been added to your list and thank them for joining.

Hook
Entice your subscribers with an alluring offer they can't refuse and cannot wait to share with their friends. Free items are always the best, whether it's a drink, appetizer, bag, or whatever you believe drives another visit. Appeal to the customer's sense of value, as illustrated below.

"Thanks for signing up. To receive 25% off your first order, present this text at the checkout."

How Often Will You Communicate?
Tell your subscribers upfront how often you will send messages. Alerting customers to the frequency of your text messages will put their mind at ease and adhere to best practices.

How to Opt-out
Include in your text messages how recipients can opt-out. I know, we really don't want them to ever opt-out but savvy customers will notice if you leave this option out. Not including an easy, simple way to opt-out will confuse recipients and, ultimately, make them unhappy with your brand. Here's an example of a simple opt-out.

"Thank you for your text. You have successfully subscribed to our mailing list. To opt-out, reply STOP."

How to Keep Your Text-based Subscribers

In the fickle world we live in, where loyalty is as fleeting as the attention of a goldfish, it's critical to maintain and grow your customer database, while limiting the potential for those who might opt-out. How do you do this? Simple. Continue to provide irresistible offers or provide valuable content recipients can't get anywhere else. While you don't have to continue to give away freebies after you have your customers hooked, the fact is you want them to stay hooked. Here are a few recommendations.

Don't provide offers recipients can get through email, magazines or off TV. Text message offers should be **unique and exclusive**. Unique and exclusive offers also help build your database through word of mouth. When you send out exclusive shop-early sales event notices, member-only, or buy-one-get-one (BOGO) offers and contests, not only will you keep the customers you have, you'll gain more as your customers relay your offers to their friends and family. Notice I threw in an exclusive notice. Not every text marketing message has to be about money and savings. Sometimes, it's the element of time that drives customers to respond, such as a "9 a.m. to 11 a.m. preview" or special. In short, if you make your SMS customers feel special, you'll increase customer loyalty.

Make sure the offers you send are **easy to use**. Don't make subscribers print out the coupon to redeem it. Showing the text or reading the coupon code to the checkout clerk should be all the work subscribers have to do. If you make calls to action too difficult, subscribers will ignore your offers and most likely opt-out.

Do your research. Remember, texting is no longer about teens and 20-somethings. You now have an older demographic with different wants and needs. Casinos, especially those outside of Las Vegas, are notoriously slow movers when it comes to marketing innovation and mobile technologies. On my way to meet with a casino in Kansas, I noticed a truck ahead swerving from lane to lane. It was fairly early in the morning and I hoped this driver wasn't already drunk or still drunk from the night before. As I cautiously pulled beside the truck, I looked over and noticed a 60-plus year old man texting on his phone.

When I reached the casino and shared my experience with the marketing director and director of IT, they explained that their primary demographic (age 65 and over) discovered texting because their grandchildren practically forced them into using it to communicate. Texting was the only way grandma and grandpa could talk to their grandchildren. Grandkids no longer talked on the phone or sent emails. That's so mom and dad's era.

The point is to **know your audience**. Research what appeals to them. Keep an eye on your redemption rate and opt-out metrics to develop a laser focus on what works and what doesn't. Increase your ROI by building an effective mobile marketing campaign and look like a rock star.

Check your tone. Humor is the first thing that comes to my mind, but be careful using it. Remember that people cannot hear voice inflections in a text, so the opportunity to be misconstrued is big. How many times have you sent something you thought was funny to someone and they completely misunderstood what you meant? The same can be true here. If your brand isn't about humor then don't use it. You can turn people off quickly and see your unsubscribe rate rocket. Sonic Drive-In is a brand that can get away with some humor. Sonic's TV advertisements using the two guys wise-cracking about a new food or drink item employs humor quite effectively. Of course, the "two guys" also happen to be professional comedians and the campaign itself is years old, making it practically a staple in the world of TV advertising.

The same can be said for using high-dollar words and risking coming off as aloof. Don't turn your customers off by talking down to them or appearing to go over their heads. In addition, watch how hard you "push" your offer. Pushing too hard can come off as desperate and have your brand looking like a sleazy used car salesman. It bears repeating: Knowing your audience and demographics is critical to developing messages that resonate with customers and compels them to respond.

Sometimes failure is out of your hands. A natural disaster or catastrophic world event can side-track any campaign if they happen to coincide. You can put together the most brilliant texting campaign, only to have it snuffed out by bad customer service or bad customer experiences. Defective products, unclean stores, and a rude wait staff can leave a bad taste in your customer's mouth that will force them to unsubscribe. If you're listening and doing surveys, you can address these problems and work to keep your subscribers by letting them know you're addressing these issues. You can also use your texting platform to gather quick survey information.

Personalization

Personalization is the ultimate way to keep customers connected with your brand. Personalization is so important that it deserves its own section. If you can't tell, I like statistics. Statistics provide a breakdown of what works, what doesn't, and where problems lay. In a recent Direct Marketing Association (DMA) survey, 70% of the sample revealed that customers had responded to a marketing text message. The DMA added that only 30% of those surveyed responded to a marketing email. A Cisco survey reported 58% of customers said they would be willing to share their information (even clothing sizes) *if the content was personalized*. According to a September 2013 research report by Forbes Insights, more than three-quarters of U.S. business-to-consumer customers saw the benefit of trading personal information for more relevant discounts and offers, and 62% were willing to do so in return for personalized offers.

Personalization = Effectiveness = Success

Personalization is effective. A recent Infosys survey reported that 78% of consumers are more likely to be repeat customers if a retailer provides personalized offers. Fact is, your customers expect a personalized experience. With text message marketing, you have the means and opportunity through two-way communication to get to know your customers' preferences.

Personalized email is 57% more effective at generating customer return and produces six times the transaction rates and revenue, according to an Experian Marketing Services study. Yet, only 13% of companies deliver a personalized mobile experience per ExactTarget. This should be your personal call-to-action. You can jump ahead of the curve if you start delivering personalized content to your subscribers. If Joe only buys men's clothing from your location, don't send him a coupon for women's clothes.

Most text message marketing campaigns start with an off-the-rack communication. The communication is generic and covers all bases. Unless the new subscriber is an existing customer in your CRM, you don't know anything about them. There is little else you can do other than taking a one-size-fits-all approach. Using keywords can help you figure out more about your customers' preferences. For example, placing multiple keywords around the store in different departments can provide personal customer intelligence: Text MEN to 55678, text SPORTS to 55678 or text WOMEN to 55678. These keyword-based offers can narrow down preferences until you learn more about your customers.

In today's world of data-driven enterprises, it's important to segment your customers by their preferences. This helps you, as the marketer, develop content that is relevant to each segment. In the end, this helps you maintain your subscribers and builds loyalty. Segment your customers based on their profile, preferences and locations for one-to-one personalization of your texts. Integrate this information with existing customer data systems whenever possible.

At the most basic level, you must look at two segments: new customers and existing customers. Each segment has completely different customer journeys, different experiences, paths to purchase and needs. New customers are easier to get on board with your text messaging program. Existing customers need more and better incentives to bring them into the fold. Leverage your existing customer communication channels like email or social media to introduce them to better incentives when they subscribe to your text message offers.

How Often Should You Text?

I love Italian food, especially a good marina sauce, and I'm not shy about sharing that fact. My friends know it. My family knows it. My co-workers know it. One year around my birthday, I was given the opportunity to share several meals with friends and family. Unfortunately, they took the whole Italian thing a little too far. After having Italian at least once a day for five straight days, I never wanted to see another tomato sauce again.

While text marketing is a great way to speak directly to your customers on everything from upcoming sales to free offers to grand openings to exclusive sneak peeks, there is definitely such a thing as "too much of a good thing."

You will hear many different takes on this. I've spoken to one industry "expert" who suggests the general rule-of-thumb to keep customers satisfied is sending no more than one text per day. I will respectfully disagree by saying any more than once or twice a week is too much. While some studies show that marketers can send as many as 10-12 texts per month without losing a major portion of subscribers, I would start on the lower end before working up in frequency.

The key to determine how often you should text is testing your frequency since each customer group is different. Run the same type of deals and change the frequency. Some recipients will unsubscribe or opt-out. That's fine. It's going to happen no matter what you do. Whatever the frequency that results in the least amount of people unsubscribing or opting out is the right frequency. A word of caution, though: Don't change your frequency *and* your deal/offer at the same time or you won't get a good read to determine what the right mix is for either.

There are, of course, exceptions to this. Special events, for example, will necessitate more frequent communication with your customers. Don't be scared of this. If the message is strong and the value is obvious and worthwhile, your subscribers generally won't mind an extra text or two if the content contains value to them.

Make Your SMS Marketing More Viral

People enjoy forwarding great offers or interesting news. SMS makes this easy for them to do. Since viral marketing can explode a campaign and ignite your brand, it pays to maximize the probability that your message will be forwarded on.

I was amazed when Redbox changed its marketing tactics. I understand rewarding customers differently, depending on their usage and loyalty. However, the timeliness of the offers I received as a customer didn't match the time or day I wanted to watch a movie rental. I liked the offers my friend received better. In the early days of Redbox and its promotions, my friend would send me the code she'd received. I'd enter the same code and get my movies for the night. I generally ran late to return the movies so Redbox still got my money. Unfortunately, Redbox got smart to this idea and decided to tie the coupon code specifically to the recipient's account, which meant my friend and I were not able to share offers anymore. I felt slighted and discriminated against. I can't remember the last time I rented a movie from Redbox.

The following are some ways to help you increase your "viral quotient."

Include a "Share" prompt. It's easy to overlook a simple thing like asking your customers to share the text with a friend or family. Remind them to spread the word. Make sure they know it's OK to send the offer to anyone they want. The most forwarded texts are coupons, entertainment content and greeting cards.

Incentivize sharing. Motivate your customers with rewards for passing along your text. Track this with coupon codes to enter on websites or at your point-of-sale. If you're conducting a sweepstakes, give customers extra entries for each friend they sign up. Don't do these too often or they will lose their effectiveness. Subscribers and especially their friends tend to grow tired and wary of the share factor.

SMS Example:

Joe.com! Thanks for Joining, Get 10 friends to text your code SEG2FG to 12123 and get a $25 Gift Card! STOP2end Msg&DataRatesMayAply

FWD to Friends: Hey, help me get rewarded. Text my code SEG2FG to 12123 and I get a $25 Gift Card! U can get a code too! STOP2end Msg&DataRatesMayAply

Give Gifts. Send special coupons around the holidays or during special occasions when subscribers can share with a friend (two-for-one) or send to a friend. Have the friend show the forwarded message to your staff to redeem the offer.

Different Ways to Use SMS

Text-to-Win Contest

Caribou Coffee, the second largest specialty coffee and espresso retailer in the U.S., planned to open a new store in Illinois. The company developed a text-to-win campaign to build buzz around the opening. Customers could enter via SMS for a chance to win a prize package. To participate, consumers entered the keyword OAKBROOK to the short code 70626 for the chance to win free drinks for one year at the new Caribou Coffee location. This tactic built Caribou's subscriber base allowing the company to push out future relevant offers and deals.

Reese's Peanut Butter Cups launched a text-to-win promotion for a chance to score tickets to the 2013 NCAA Men's Basketball

Tournament. Customers were encouraged to text back for a chance to win one of the tickets. Reese's also gathered email addresses in the process to gain another channel to communicate with its customers. Customers could then send a link to the Reese's mobile site where they could keep up to date on the tournament.

Starbucks launched a trivia content promotion where customers could opt-in to answer a trivia question. The first correct answers won a CD of the soundtrack from the Great Gatsby film.

Coupons/Offers

According to a study conducted by ABI Research, 52% of consumers would use mobile coupons to obtain discounts at local stores. Go Mobile suggests that redemption rates of mobile coupons are as much as 10 times higher than those of printed coupons. This trend indicates that mobile coupon offers are a valuable tactic to add to your marketing quiver. But how do you go about doing this? What kinds of offers are most effective?

A Cellit survey found that buy-one-get-one (BOGO) mobile coupons were clearly more popular among young consumers, with 68% preferring them to other forms of coupons. This is more desirable to a percentage discount. When crafting your message, make sure it's brief and instructs the subscriber how to use the coupon. Use personal, friendly language when at all possible.

Avoid coupon abuse
1. Include expiration dates.
2. Limit the number of uses. For example, the first 50 people to use this coupon…

3. Train staff to verify the coupon number. If the coupon comes from a number that isn't your short code, your staff can politely ask the customer to subscribe to receive the coupon, then redeem it. If it's passed along from a friend or family, the number will be different
4. Deliver the coupon via mobile web page. The text can contain a link to a web page that displays the ad with a bar code that can be scanned. This will, most likely, restrict the number of people who use the coupon to smartphone users with a data plan. 7-Eleven, an international chain of convenience stores, used a web page with a coupon during its 2012 Slurpee voting campaign that customers could redeem while in the store. The coupon expired 15 minutes after validation

Types of mobile offers
Responsys published a study in December 2013 in which it asked consumers, "if you were to receive the following types of offers on your mobile device, how likely is each to trigger an action on your part?" Responsys separated the intent into three categories: likely, neither likely nor unlikely, and unlikely. Overwhelmingly, the price-based offers were the most likely at 66%. Time-sensitive offers and location-based offers were close to each other at 52% and 50%, respectively. Product-based offers and similar product-based offers came in near the bottom, with a very general offer intended for the masses in dead last place.

Time-sensitive and location-based offers evoke a sense of urgency which motivates consumers to act. I would hazard to say that while consumers responded near 50%, I think their actions may prove equal or higher than a strict pricing-based offer. People, forget about the pricing offers if there isn't a sense of urgency to the deal. Combining the two would be the best of both worlds.

Coupon effectiveness example: Dairy Queen – Texas style
A 27-location Dairy Queen franchisee wanted to deliver new services that connected customers with their brand. The franchisee's primary campaign goals were to build brand awareness, increase revenue and provide its 27 locations with marketing support. imobilize media executed a 1:1 digital marketing approach that deployed a mobile SMS coupon campaign supported with newspaper inserts, direct mail, posters, POP and social media messages to anchor Dairy Queen's call-to-action and integrate the SMS campaign with additional marketing tactics.

Dairy Queen tracked the campaign's effectiveness and discovered the following results:

- Customer opt-ins grew 125% every week during the 30-day campaign
- Coupon redemption rates came in between 32-48% across all 27 locations on one 48-hour time stamp
- Retention rates (the number of people that did not opt-out and continued to receive future text message marketing) came in at 96.2%
- DQ and imobilize media measured the ROI at more than 1000% for the campaign

Surveys
Surveys are an underutilized tool and can be very powerful when done correctly. Surveys provide invaluable insight into your business, customer habits and preferences. They open up a line of communication between you and your customer. They

also emphasize that you value your customers' opinions. I'm not talking about a 40-question, 20-minute survey. That's too much. However, five or six key questions that provide immediate and actionable insight can change the face of your business.

Think about it. Your customers can fill out the survey in a couple of minutes, at most. You receive immediate feedback from the purchase while it's fresh on their mind and before any changes in attitude. Reach them before someone cuts them off in line or they go somewhere else. This information can be sent to your management team who can either give everyone high praise or find out who's having the bad day affecting customers negatively.

Polling or Voting

While the mechanics of polling are similar to surveys, I separate them into two different categories. Yes, you are asking a question to a group of people. However, polling should be much simpler and possibly contain only one question. Surveys can dive into the customer experience or service extremely well. Polling can be made fun. Say, for example, you own a pizza restaurant. You have a few ideas for some new pizza combinations but are uncertain if your customers will love them as much as you and more importantly, will order them. This is a fantastic example of what SMS polling can do for you.

- Place a sign in various spots in your restaurant or place of business. We'll continue with the pizza example but you can envision how this could work in your own business. Let's say the sign reads "Which pizza should we add next month? Phlliy Steak, Chicken Alfredo or

Hawaiian Paradise? Cast your vote by texting PHILLY or CHICKEN or PARADISE to 55678
- You receive responses from your customers
- You text them back letting them know the results and when the pizza will be on the menu and available to order
- You reward them with a promo code to receive $5 off the new pizza

Paper and phone polling is still in use, but let's look at some advantages of SMS polling:

- Paper and phone ballots can be miscalculated or even sabotaged
- Paper ballots can be lost
- Paper and phone ballots require personnel to gather and count the votes
- SMS polling can be launched and conducted anywhere
- SMS polling is eco-friendly
- SMS polling can lead to new subscriptions
- SMS polling can lead to new marketing channels

Sponsorship Activation

Use available mobile media assets, including bounce-back messages and Text-to-Screen ad space to sell sponsorships and generate new revenue streams. Team up with large advertisers to promote voting an MVP of the game or send fan pictures via MMS and put it up on the Jumbotron.

Example: Oklahoma State University (OSU) Fan Activation

Cowboy Sports Properties, a division of Learfield Sports managing the multi-media rights for Oklahoma State University

Athletic Department, wanted to build a closer connection with fans. The company teamed up with imobilize media, Arby's, Dr. Pepper and COX Cable to marry mobile, social and in-stadium/arena video boards. Utilizing mobile phone cameras, MMS and email, the company (and ultimately the team) received hundreds of tailgating and game-day pics from fans. The best photos were featured on the video boards throughout the game. Exclusive offers were sent via SMS to the winners whose photos were included in the video vignettes.

The success of the program drew national advertising support from Arby's and Dr. Pepper. Management watched as OSU brand awareness increased as a result of fusing several mediums and placing them in the hands of college students and Oklahoma State University fans.

Donations

Donations can be made to non-profit organizations by texting a keyword to a specific SMS short code. The process is the same as premium SMS messages where the donation of $5 to $10 appears on the donor's monthly carrier bill. The number of donations per month per customer is limited. If you are the charity, understand up front how much of the donation gets eaten up by service provider's fees.

The guidelines for charitable donations via SMS are strict. As a not-for-profit, charities must go through an intermediary organization to manage a SMS donation campaign. The charity must complete an application process to become a participating nonprofit. Next, the organization will choose a short code, negotiate terms with the provider, then finalize and promote their text campaign. Not every not-for-profit can sign up for a donation text message service, and not every text message platform can support the service. The complexity involved keeps spammers at bay and the public from being taken advantage of.

After the 7.0 magnitude earthquake hit Haiti in 2010, close to $5 million in donations were generated by small donors only 44 hours later

Hurricane Sandy in 2013 was one of the largest recorded hurricanes to hit the Atlantic. Of the millions of dollars raised to help victims of this tragedy, 20% were raised from text message donations.

Support Hurricane Sandy Relief Efforts. Text REDCROSS to 90999 to donate $10

The Red Cross has enjoyed the simplicity of using text messaging to raise money for years. For the donor, the process is easy, quick and anyone with a mobile phone can participate. No credit cards, check or cash is required at the time of donation. The donation is simply added to the giver's monthly phone bill.

Send VIP Offers

The best performing SMS marketing campaigns are ones where the recipients believe they're receiving added value or some substantial benefit, such as exclusive content or high-value mobile coupons. If you send exclusive offers to your mobile marketing customer list, you'll likely increase customer loyalty. You can also leverage brand affinity by inviting your VIP customers to share your offers with their friends if they join your list as well.

The Las Vegas Hotel and Casino tied its SMS campaign to its loyalty club by offering prizes to visitors who opted in to receive the hotel and casino's marketing messages. The visitors were then upgraded to an A-List Player's Club membership. The simple campaign increased membership by 13%.

Best Practices

Spam-Free Zone
Nobody likes spam, especially on their cell phone. If you're sending out multiple messages each day, sending out sales and non-informative messages, your subscribers are going to consider this as spam and quickly opt-out. Remember, text message marketing is a permission-only based form of communication. Any time you send a marketing text message to someone who has not specifically opted-in to your program, you are spamming.

Timeliness
A good rule-of-thumb is to send text messages between 9 a.m. and 8 p.m. Any other times will be unwelcome to late risers or early sleepers. Another good way to select the best time(s) to send text messages is to look at your website analytics. Determine what times of the day or night your website is visited by mobile devices and send the messages at those peak times. Don't send breakfast coupons at 3 p.m. and dinner coupons at 8 a.m. Scheduling your message is simple logic that we sometimes forget. Send relevant, personalized messages when subscribers want them and at times when they can take action.

Call-to-Action
There are only so many characters you can include in a text message so make them count, but don't forget to include a call-to-action. Be sure to add a reply option, location address to visit, website address, coupon to present or a number to click-to-call.

URL Shorteners
To conserve character count for the most important content, utilize URL shortening services like bit.ly and ow.ly to shorten your URL.

Easy Opt-Out
We want every customer to stay with us forever. Unfortunately that's not going to happen. Make it easy for subscribers to opt-out.

Local
If you're a large company with several locations across the country, make your content personal and appear local. Also, time the message deployment correctly. Don't forget the difference in time zones.

Offer Expiration
Include a sense of urgency to your offer. Don't leave the message open-ended. You want subscribers to take action sooner rather than later when all will be forgotten and they go to a competitor because they forgot your offer.

Creativity
Get inspired and inspire your customers. Be creative in your campaign to make subscribers fall in love with you. Straight couponing only works so well. Try techniques like gamification,

MMS, emoticons, social sharing and share with a friend. If your subscribers have web-enabled mobile phones, have fun with gamification techniques like scratch offs, roulette wheels and Match 3.

PETA uses emoticons to tie in love with <3 instead of "Y" for yes. This creative use of two characters falls in line with PETA's message and platform. Utilize MMS to share 30-second videos or pictures to mix up standard messaging. If you're going to use MMS, make sure you—not your subscribers—are paying the messaging costs or you may have a revolt on your hands.

Geo-fencing

When are customers more apt to use a coupon or redeem a deal? When they receive a text while sitting on the couch? Or when they are near your store? Customers might be slightly concerned when receiving offers while they're in the vicinity (Big Brother is watching). However, it really makes the most sense to send offers when customers are most likely to use them – when they're close. I'm not necessarily going to immediately jump off my couch and run to the store when I get a text sent to me in the middle of watching my favorite show. However, I might change direction while I'm out shopping if I'm hit with a good offer.

Not while I'm driving. Texting while driving is a social hot button that you need to be aware of and maintain the best interest of your customers. You cannot get them in the store if they are filling out a police report on a wreck because they looked at your text instead of the car ahead of them.

Thus geo-fencing. With the ability to triangulate a cell phone's coordinates through the use of cell towers, the carrier pings cell phones of consumers in the campaign database. If the cellular triangulation locates the consumer phone within the geo-fencing area, the mobile marketing platform receives notification that the consumer is within range – triggering a text message. The consumer is sent relevant call-to-action text messaging and the consumer can use the text to redeem the deal. A follow-up text can be sent to the consumer, building brand loyalty and capture the data and analyze the sales for ROI on the campaign.

Of course, you can only apply geo-fencing if the customer has given you permission. To pull this off effectively, you must build trust with your customers and provide them with valuable offers to make the trade-off of knowing their location worth it.

A deeper look into the steps of geo-fencing reveal there are a few more details into this process. First, let's talk about carrier pings. Not all carriers will or can ping their customers. Next, there is an additional cost to pings. These pings can range from $0.02 to $0.06 per ping, depending on volume. These pings have to be issued with enough frequency to approximate the consumer's real-time location. This can add up quickly. Using $0.04 per ping with 1,000 customers, and assuming the marketer only does one ping per minute between the hours of 10 a.m. and 6 p.m., results in $0.04 x 1,000 customers x 8 hours x 60 minutes/hour for a total cost of $19,200. While the cost increases, you generally achieve a higher ROI without having to use GPS and restrict your marketing to smartphones.

To reduce the cost, restaurants might only request pings during lunch and dinner, reducing the hours and number of pings dramatically. Retail locations may only ping after 5 p.m. and on weekends. If you try to ping with less frequency, you run the risk of the consumer passing through the geo-fence without receiving your entire message. To combat this, you may want to increase your geo-fence. This, however, runs the risk of customers receiving the message from too far away and annoyed that they're receiving messages that aren't within a reasonable distance. You can see how geo-fencing can get tricky really fast.

An alternative to geo-fencing may be to segment your list by ZIP code to send targeted messages. While the delivery may not be in "real-time" and the subscriber may not be in the area of your store, segmenting by ZIP code can provide a more cost effective solution.

Again, I do not advocate texting and driving. Don't use geo-fencing for two-way communication. Make sure the timing of the offer is such that it doesn't force a subscriber to respond to the offer immediately. Texting while driving increases the likeliness of a car crash 23 times the norm. Texting while driving has become the number one driving distraction for many people.

You may decide to avoid geo-fencing for this reason. You may decide to require two consecutive pings within the geo-fenced area to avoid drivers and focus on shoppers in the area. Get creative and promote safe text message marketing.

Get Your Employees Involved

In all likelihood, one employee probably heads up your SMS marketing. This person creates, manages, sends and receives messages—all of which can be done at a computer or, sometimes, just a smartphone. However, if you want to get the most out of your campaign, it's a team effort.

We see businesses constantly touting their Facebook and/or Twitter accounts. Do the same with your SMS campaign. Train your employees, at every level, to speak intelligently and with excitement about your program. Help them understand that this is a product to sell just like the products on the shelf. Show them how to sign up customers for the program, what the benefits are, and bring passion to the cause. Incentivize them to promote your SMS campaign in the store and outside the building walls.

Get to Know Your Subscribers. But Not All at Once

The personal aspect of text message marketing is unparalleled when compared to other forms of marketing. The two-way communication inherent in text message marketing provides the ability to ask questions and gain more knowledge about your subscribers. Facilitate interaction to build relationships with your customers. Don't hit them repeatedly over the head with the same marketing and advertising.

In today's world, data is paramount. The better you know your customers, the better you can serve them with personalized offers according to their preferences. While text message marketing enables you to ask questions and build profiles around each subscriber, it's not in your best interest to do this all at once. Don't ask a long continual stream of questions about your subscribers' lives and expect them not to unsubscribe. Additionally, provide the incentive to share. Just like you provide your subscribers with an incentive to join your text message club, provide them with incentives to give you information. Determine the value of the information you request and incentivize accordingly.

Guidelines from the Mobile Marketing Association (MMA)

We have been subjected to a slew of political spam, scam subscriptions, infected phones and phish for financial data for what seems a long while. This has resulted in consumers becoming more hostile, resistant and distrustful of all mobile marketing messages. The volume and content we are subjected to nowadays deter and undermine effectiveness. To discourage brands and SMS platforms who abuse text message marketing, marketers, platforms, carriers, businesses and governing bodies are taking action to ensure consumer protection going forward. These actions include, but are not limited to, $500/text message fine and being blacklisted and dropped from distributing messages to carriers.

Get Permission

A Direct Marketing Association survey revealed that 43% of respondents have received "unsolicited SMS spam promoting accident claims or mis-selling financial services." According to AdaptiveMobile, more than 148 million spam texts are received by British customers every month. Research indicates that spam text messages grew 45% in 2011 to 4.5 billion messages, globally. While that is 0.2% of all the text messages delivered worldwide, the numbers are still staggering and—unfortunately—growing. On a global basis, individuals and businesses don't have the legislation or the governing bodies to impede the growth of spam.

Keep in mind that some people don't have unlimited text plans or service. This being the case, unsolicited text messages can cost consumers as much as $0.20/message depending on the carrier and data plan, thus forcing customers to "buy" something just by opening the text message. For this reason it is imperative that formal permission or "strict consent" be obtained before sending any text message. Getting phone numbers off contracts, invoices or business cards from a fish bowl **does not** constitute permission. Nor does it give you permission to send a text message asking someone to join your text program.

Marketers who have latched onto SMS view the potential it offers as not only a valuable form of two-way communication and intelligence-gathering, but a smart addition to a new or existing marketing plan. When used appropriately, adhering to all privacy regulations, SMS is a trusted, quickest read and most frequently read form of electronic communication today. Unfortunately, spammers have also discovered these benefits, not to mention unsuspecting companies that make uneducated choices when selecting a text message marketing platform. Terrorizing customers with unsolicited, unsubscribed-to messages and advertisements threatens the growth of what has proven to be a simple, inexpensive, results-oriented marketing tactic. Most unfortunately, it only takes a few text-message recipients who did not subscribe to receive offers via their smartphones to spoil any future opportunities to reach them. Like they say, one bad apple…

Incoming communication to auto-responders are useful tools that provide immediate information to customers. This information could include your location, hours, daily special, wait time, etc. However, this does not constitute permission to send text marketing messages to the inbound communicator. An auto-responder is a one-time communication that, generally, does not contain the proper opt-in language. Be sure you utilize auto-responders appropriately or risk the wrath of your customers or prospective customers.

Keep Records

Ensure you keep records of all opt-in **and** opt-out transmissions. I recently learned of an unsavory character who threatened a text message platform for text messages he continued to receive after opting-out. At a fine of $500 per text, this unnecessary cost, due to poor recordkeeping, would add up very quickly. Fortunately, the platform kept records of all opt-ins, including the complainant, and his failure to opt-out. The threats ceased immediately. Retain all records of consent/agreement for a minimum of six months after subscribers have opted-out. I would suggest that you retain all opt-in and opt-out records even longer. We live in an extremely litigious society and one lawsuit can derail all of your best-laid plans

STOP Means STOP

Yes, this seems like a simple directive by a subscriber, but you'd be surprised by the number of businesses who either unwittingly or willfully ignore these requests, or simply do not reconcile their records every day to act upon a subscriber's request to STOP sending them texts.

Coca-Cola® found this out the hard way. Consumers were unable to opt-on of receiving text messages. Not being able to opt-out is a violation of the Telephone Consumer Protection Act (TCPA). Subscribers of the MyCokeRewards text-to-win campaign attempted to text STOP but were unsuccessful and continued to receive unwanted text messages. The lesson learned here? When a subscriber opts-out, you must cease and desist from sending them texts. A Federal Communications Commission (FCC)-issued declaratory ruling has opened the door for one additional text (the "follow up" confirmation) to verify subscribers want to stop receiving your text messages, but that is it. The follow-up confirmation text message must be sent within five minutes of receiving the opt-out request and cannot include any marketing or promotional information.

Thanks to Barclays settling a class action suit for more than $8 million, a rash of companies has been threatened with lawsuits, including American Express, Twitter and Facebook. The industry won victory as the FCC declared in a recent ruling confirming that companies and organizations may legally send a final, one-time text to confirm receipt of a consumer's opt-out request of a text messaging program.

Audit
The Coca-Cola debacle is a great example of why audits should be regularly conducted. Don't put the blame on or try to sue the platform; this has already been shot down in court. Your business is the responsible party. To avoid expensive litigation and gone-forever customers, simply run weekly audits on all of your text messaging initiatives and responses, including unsubscribes, opt-ins and opt-outs. Then ensure the subscriber's decision has been accommodated. This is the only way to head off potential failures in the system and avoid costly lawsuits and brand-damage. Otherwise, good luck keeping your job.

When proper, legal procedures aren't followed, the brand and the business receive the public black eye and suffer a big dent in the pocket book.

Secure Your Customers' Data
Customer data security breaches inside text messaging platforms hasn't been an issue so far, but I believe it's closer than most think. Hackers are everywhere, with the time and intelligence to steal private and confidential information at every opportunity.   Protecting your customers' information is paramount. When choosing a platform, security from unauthorized use, disclosure or access should be of utmost importance and should be standard issue for all text messaging platforms. Utilize every protection means possible to keep your data from becoming comprised (Remember Target?). This will keep your brand image clean and clear from being dragged through the mud and suspect for both new and existing customers.

Select Your Words Carefully
When describing your text message programs, be aware of the word "FREE." You cannot use the word "FREE" to entice customers to join your program unless the texts and program truly are free to the end-user (FTEU) with all supported carriers. So as not to confuse or mislead customers, services also cannot be promoted in association with the word "free." You must use the phrase "Msg & data rates may apply" to any campaign that is not FTEU.

Help and Terms
HELP can be provided in lieu of full customer support contact information in your advertising materials, but should be included with STOP in your follow-up opt-in confirmation

message. Terms may be disclosed via a website address and/or toll free number. To adhere to the CTIA compliance principles, abbreviated terms must be legibly displayed under the call-to-action. They must be static in TV advertisements, and the first three lines must appear above the fold on a 1024x768 screen. At minimum, these terms must disclose the product description and quantity, program identification, message and data rates may apply, links to privacy policy, and opt-out instructions in **bold typeface**. Comprehensive terms must be featured on a static website.

Advertising Your Text Message Program

When advertising your text message program in print ads, signage or television, you must include a few specifics that are mandated by both the mobile phone carriers and the Mobile Marketing Association's U.S. Consumer Best Practices.

1. Describe the program. You are required to state specifically what the subscriber is opting-in to (i.e. to receive coupons, specials, updates, or other content)
2. "Msg&Data rates may apply". This exact phrase is required below the call to action within the advertisement if not FTEU. Most text message platforms automatically add the phrase in for you
3. Provide a response means for HELP, such as a website or phone number, which can be replaced with "T&C, text HELP"
4. Opt-out instructions, such as a link to opt-out or a means to Text STOP
5. Frequency of SMS campaign. Make it clear to the subscriber at the outset how many text messages they can expect to receive per month

Additional conditions also must be met when advertising to children or youth under the age of 21, advertising alcohol or tobacco products, or advertising sweepstakes and premium text programs. Take a close and hard look at the legal aspects for these required conditions and only work with companies that understand the legal ramifications inside and out.

While the brands usually are not in direct fault, they are hit with large fines for the technical issues of the SMS platform they use. To avoid fines (and the negative public relations that can follow them):

- Choose wisely when selecting a texting platform
- Protect yourself by regularly performing your own audits
- Know the FCC rulings (like the Telephone Consumer Protection Act described in the next section)
- Be aware of the CTIA compliance principles
- And finally, implement the Mobile Marketing Association's (MMA) best practices before you start any text messaging campaign

Telephone Consumer Protection Act – "TCPA" (the other text messaging rules)

The TCPA was passed into law in 1991 and is policed by the Federal Communications Commission (FCC). Beginning October 16, 2013, prior express written consent is required for all text messages sent to cell phones for marketing and sales purposes.

In compliance with the E-SIGN Act, electronic or digital forms of signatures are acceptable via email, website form, text message, telephone keypress or voice recording. Included in this law, the "established business relationship" exemption for pre-recorded telemarketing calls to residential landlines was eliminated. However, there never was an "established business relationship" exemption for text messaging. The TCPA provides for either actual damages or statutory damages that can range from $500 to $1,500 per unsolicited message.

For all text subscribers after October 16, 2013, marketers must comply with the following:

- Express signed consent from all opt-ins to receive text marketing correspondence from your business. Consent can be made in writing, or electronic or digital forms that fall in compliance with the E-SIGN Act
- Correspondence requesting consent must state "consent to get text not required OR condition of purchase"
- Provide opt-out and help instructions
- Indicate frequency of texts
- Indicate that messages may come from senders
- Disclose possible carrier costs and fees
- If directing to a landing page, any check box fields must be left unchecked
- Consent sent must match that requested by the initial opt-in

For all members within a business's current database, marketers must comply with the following:

- Request new consent from all members within a database who did not previously do so
- Share disclosures
- Send a compliant text to re-establish opt-in

The following is an example of requesting new consent:

Joe Alerts: Reply Y to get exclusive coupons/alerts from Joe. Up to 8msg/mo. Txt HELP for help. STOP to stop. Msg&DataRatesMayAply www.joe.com/privacy

This message starts with a clear indicator of the source, Joe. Using Y, instead of YES, saves character count. The message discloses the text frequency; explains how to get help or stop future messages; identifies rates that may apply; and provides a link to privacy information. The only thing the message didn't include was the statement that a purchase was not necessary. It's easy to see that compliance with new regulations may well require more than one text.

Track Your SMS Marketing Campaigns

Let's say you've developed your SMS campaign. You've complied with all the text messaging rules and regulations and customers have signed up to receive your texts. Now what? Like any good marketing campaign, it's time to determine how you will track its effectiveness. An effective campaign can mean different things to different businesses, whether it be a sharp increase in traffic to your website or place of business (brand awareness); increased product or service sales; coupon redemption; giveaways or sweepstakes participation; offer sharing; or database growth. Think through your campaign before sending out the first marketing text to determine what your goals are and how you will measure achieving them. Analyzing data can also bring insight into responses you may not see.

Mobile Carrier Data

The text message platform provider you select will provide important data points that enable marketers to see where customers have opted in, the text message open rate, and the carrier a recipient's cell number is associated with.

Mobile Analytics Data

Analyzing mobile analytics enable marketers to identify year-over-year growth, the number of opt-outs during a selected timeframe, the effectiveness of specific keywords tied to different campaigns, media channel effectiveness, and more.

Google Analytics

Embedding a URL link into your text message that drives consumers to a special landing page can also help track campaign effectiveness. Google Analytics (and other services that track website metrics) provides data on the number of people who clicked through to the landing page. If you want to drive recipients to a product page in your site, add an ID to the URL to track where they're coming from. While it's possible to track visits from a mobile phone, the information will be muddy as you will not be able to determine if the visits are coming from your text, someone browsing your website, or someone who has the page bookmarked on their mobile device.

Coupon Tracking
To track the effectiveness and redemption rate of text coupons, add a coupon code that can be entered on the POS at customer checkout.

Call Tracking
Monitor the number of people who call in response to a text by setting up a special phone number that is dedicated to a specific campaign.

Split or A/B Testing
Tracking consumer response to a marketing campaign is critical to determine its ultimate success or failure but also vital to assessing your return on investment. A sale on swimsuits in August may be ideal for California women but not for those in New York. Split or A/B testing is a strategic means to test customer response to a keyword ("swimsuits") or keywords ("vacation wear") in your message content. While "swimsuits" is a perfect keyword for consumers in warmer climes, "vacation wear" may work better for those in colder locales that tend to vacation in Florida or the Caribbean. The same methodology can be applied to idioms and colloquial terms that aren't regularly used or embraced by every consumer. For example, the term "pop" (a fizzy beverage understood by many of us) is better referred to as "soda" in other geographical locations.

To test your keywords and message, split your subscribers up into separate groups then send each group your offer using different keywords. Track the usage of words like WIN or FREE to see what message relates best to your subscribers. Watch the unsubscribe rate as well as the redemption or action taken as a result of the message. Hone in on the message that is best responded to and move forward with your campaign.

NOTE: Just because a particular offer worked in your email campaign, doesn't necessarily mean it's going to work best for your text messaging campaign. Test.

Return on Investment (ROI)

One of the greatest benefits to text marketing is that, if done correctly, businesses can expect a high return on investment—something that can't be said for most traditional marketing tactics.

Let's look at an example of a client of mine, in this case a fast-food restaurant. The restaurant invested $85 per month to send out 5,000 text messages. Its subscribers for the campaign amounted to 2,500 individuals, which meant the business could send out two text messages a month to each subscriber for the $85 cost. The first text sent by the restaurant included a coupon which was tracked every time the coupon was redeemed, as well as the total purchase amount.

The results of text message number one? The coupon was redeemed 352 times with an average purchase of $11.23 for a total of $3,952.96. The average food cost, labor and overhead equated to about 45% of the investment, or $1,778.83, resulting in a profit of $2,174.13. Even with an $85 hard investment, that's nearly a 26:1 ratio with a 14% redemption rate. Bonus prize? A second round of text messages "on the house" using the rest of the initial messaging investment.

The Significance of the Unsubscribe

After a positive ROI conversation, let's now look at the economic impact of unsubscribers.

- With each customer a business attracts, the business pays a cost to acquire that customer. This may include additional staff, overtime, new equipment, other capital expenditures and, of course, all marketing and advertising required to introduce your products or services and entice customers to experience your brand.
- Once customers are acquired, businesses pay a re-marketing cost to keep touch points with those customers. Part of that re-marketing cost, in this context, is text message marketing.
- Over time, we can subtract the cost of customer acquisition and re-marketing from all purchases past, present and future related to that customer, and we have what's known as customer lifetime value (CLV).

The higher the CLV, the better businesses are marketing. The problem is that every time a customer unsubscribes to our text messages, our marketing costs go up as we must now either acquire a new customer or try to re-engage the old customer. This is one reason why it's important to begin text message marketing with a lower frequency and increase over time rather than the other way around. Tests have shown that sending a text message once every two days resulted in a 40% monthly unsubscribe rate.

Let's look at an example of the cost of unsubscribes. We have a hypothetical company that starts its text messaging campaign with one million subscribers. The company enjoys a 25% redemption rate of its coupon. The revenue of each transaction from the redemption averages $20 per ticket. The cost of sales is 10%. If we look closely at what happens to the company's gross profit as the subscription rate increases, we can clearly see the impact of the unsubscribe.

Starting Database	Unsubscribe Rate	Redemption Rate	Revenue / Redemption	Cost of Sales	Gross Profit	Unsubscribe Impact
1,000,000	0%	25%	$20	10%	$ 4,500,000	
1,000,000	1%	25%	$20	10%	$ 4,455,000	$ (45,000)
1,000,000	2%	25%	$20	10%	$ 4,410,000	$ (90,000)
1,000,000	3%	25%	$20	10%	$ 4,365,000	$ (135,000)
1,000,000	4%	25%	$20	10%	$ 4,320,000	$ (180,000)
1,000,000	5%	25%	$20	10%	$ 4,275,000	$ (225,000)

Let's take it a step further. As we all know, the impact of losing a customer is really compounded over time. If we lose 1% of subscribers each time we send out an offer, the impact is much more significant.

Database Before Content Sent	Unsubscribe Rate	Redemption Rate	Revenue / Redemption	Cost of Sales	Gross Profit	Unsubscribe Impact
1,000,000	1%	25%	$20	10%	$ 4,455,000	$ (45,000)
990,000	1%	25%	$20	10%	$ 4,410,450	$ (89,550)
980,100	1%	25%	$20	10%	$ 4,366,346	$ (133,655)
970,299	1%	25%	$20	10%	$ 4,322,682	$ (177,318)
960,596	1%	25%	$20	10%	$ 4,279,455	$ (220,545)
950,990	1%	25%	$20	10%	$ 4,236,661	$ (263,339)

Let's take a look at 2%.

Database Before Content Sent	Unsubscribe Rate	Redemption Rate	Revenue / Redemption	Cost of Sales	Gross Profit	Unsubscribe Impact
1,000,000	2%	25%	$20	10%	$ 4,410,000	$ (90,000)
980,000	2%	25%	$20	10%	$ 4,321,800	$ (178,200)
960,400	2%	25%	$20	10%	$ 4,235,364	$ (264,636)
941,192	2%	25%	$20	10%	$ 4,150,657	$ (349,343)
922,368	2%	25%	$20	10%	$ 4,067,644	$ (432,356)
903,921	2%	25%	$20	10%	$ 3,986,291	$ (513,709)

Study the 2% unsubscribe rate for a moment. What we see is an impact of more than $500,000 after five text message blasts. At 10 to 12 text messages per month, the loss is approximately

$1 million per month and could be potentially worse. This is why frequency, quality of offer, personalization, and value are so mission-critical to offset the economic impact of subscriber loss. What's more, the loss of revenue even in this hypothetical example doesn't include the cost of acquiring new customers or bringing unsubscribed customers back into the fold.

Unsubscribe rates vary by industry, so it's not possible to provide a hard and fast rule of thumb for what your specific unsubscribe rate should be. The quick serve restaurant (QSR) industry, for example, generally experiences a much higher unsubscribe rate and lower redemption rate than others. Why? There is much less loyalty among QSR customers. This is primarily because the offers aren't as appealing due to the inherent low margins in the industry. I mean, how much can you discount a 99-cent hamburger?

Examples of Successful (and Not So Successful) SMS Campaigns

Chipotle - Adventurrito

Chipotle celebrated its own birthday by holding a three-week-long treasure hunt in which the public was invited to participate. The 21st anniversary/birthday adventure offered a free burrito for a year during the first 20 days of the campaign, and grand prizes of one free burrito each week for 21 years. To receive clues for the treasure hunt, participants were asked to text a short code. In return, Chipotle texted back clues that allowed players to finish the treasure hunt faster.

Chipotle's goal was to increase brand awareness among its demographics in the fast-growing, fast casual restaurant segment. Because the campaign included a mechanism for interaction (texting short codes for clues), Chipotle leveraged the opportunity to ask players to opt-in to their SMS program. This allowed Chipotle to continue sending game clues as well as other deals and offers.

A few reasons this particular text messaging campaign worked was because Chipotle offered something of value in exchange for a mobile number. Second, the campaign itself was fresh and creative, and based on an event that connected game players with knowledge about the brand (20 years in business). Third, the game itself was well developed so that customers would continue playing. Finally, Chipotle integrated its text messaging campaign with social media platforms to grow participation and attract customers.

American Idol, The Voice, Dancing with the Stars, and Why TV Contests Depend on Text Message Marketing

Besides the fact that these reality shows are contest-based, what else do they share in common? You guessed it. They use SMS to engage viewers. For the past four years, the season finale of American Idol vote count has topped the 100 million mark, and most of those votes come through SMS. Voting strategies can be employed by virtually any business in any industry to engage existing customers, attract new ones, and increase brand awareness and sales.

The power of the voting strategy lies in engagement. After all, who doesn't have an opinion they want to share? Viewers of contest TV programming are empowered to make choices that will determine the results of the show: who stays and who goes home. The same idea can be extrapolated even further, whether it's obtaining marketing intelligence about your business's products or services, assessing brand reach, or staying on top of the needs of specific demographics. Sound like a new era for the traditional focus group? You bet.

Let's say you are the marketing director for a restaurant and want to introduce new menu items but you're a bit uncertain how those new items will be received. Offer customers the opportunity to vote for the new item they would most likely try. Use signage, posters and your website to introduce the voting campaign. Make the process easy to participate in by advertising a short code on the signage, posters and social networks. Give the campaign a shelf life of three weeks. Take off the losing item each week until only two or three are left. Add a sweepstakes of your own creation to sweeten the pie for the participant's time. Make certain you disclose that the winner(s) will be randomly drawn from the voting entries. This should trigger a higher response rate from your customers.

If you're a retailer, focus your voting campaign on determining which new brands your customers (and demographics) are raging over (and possibly buying somewhere else). You'll be surprised to discover trends and purchasing attitudes that come straight from your customers' voting choice instead of an expensive consultant.

Pirq

Pirq is a mobile app designed to help consumers discover special deals and rewards at local businesses or establishments. Pirq is essentially a local deal aggregator app, but apps like this often are caught in a chicken/egg scenario. Consumers must first sign up for the app to attract those local businesses to sign up for the service. Without signed-up consumers, businesses won't participate. Without businesses participating, consumers won't sign up. The problem isn't difficult to see.

That being said, Pirq looked to increase app installs in the real world, starting with shopping malls. They rented a gigantic indoor billboard that advertised what appeared to be a text message:

Download Now. Text "SHOP" to 33133 or visit Pirq.com

When a consumer (mall shopper) texted the code or visited the Website, Pirq replied with a link that allowed consumers to download the app to their iOS or Android device. Pirq also utilized a text-to-download file on its website homepage that enabled consumers to enter their mobile phone number in exchange for a link to download the app. The text message campaign realized a 92% click-through rate, which it should. The only reason to text to download is if you have every intention to download.

Fender Rebate

Fender, the well-known musical instrument maker, ran a promotion allowing customers who purchase select amplifiers to register for a free product rebate via SMS. While Fender still uses mail-in forms and online channels for promotion purposes, adding SMS as a redemption channel targeted teens and twenty-somethings. To redeem the rebate, the customer goes through a simple process of six text messages: name, street address, ZIP code, email address, purchased product serial number and purchase location. The simplicity of the SMS rebate tactic is particularly appealing to those who've taken advantage of rebate offers only to find the process tedious, time-consuming and sometimes even annoying. Who has the time (or inclination any more) to copy a receipt, cut out a barcode from a cardboard box and waste a stamp to mail them?

Aer Lingus

Irish airline Aer Lingus relied exclusively on email to notify passengers of flight delays or cancellations. Unfortunately, the airline reached only about 10% of their passengers. In an effort to improve relations, avoid shelling out compensation and fielding complaints, Aer Lingus implemented a SMS communications platform that dramatically increased passenger receipt of messages to 75%.

ERtexting

I love ERtexting and believe this service should be offered by all hospitals. ERtexting illustrates how an auto-responder can offer tremendous, perhaps even *life-saving* benefits, simply and easily. Imagine your child has taken a hard fall and broken her leg. She is wailing in severe pain. You need to get her to the hospital emergency room now but the injury is such that she doesn't require an ambulance. Three hospitals are located close by, but you have no idea which hospital has the shortest wait time. Here's where ERtexting comes into play: Simply text your ZIP code to the short code 437411 and—*voila!*—you receive a text reply detailing the wait times at each of the three hospitals. Convenience and value. ERtexting is a smart marketing tool for hospitals to improve their customer service perception and load balance, while offering vital information should the unexpected occur.

Healthcare

Text messaging offers numerous applications that deliver a win-win for doctors' offices, dentists, and urgent care centers.

Doctors, dentists and medical specialists can easily remind patients of upcoming appointments or instructions before the appointment, such as "no eating for 24 hours prior to your visit." Unlike the reminder email or phone call, text messaging has been shown to reduce no-shows by more than 30%. Seasonal messaging and timely messaging can also increase the number of medical visits. Alert patients to allergy and flu seasons and invite them to call and schedule their shots. Rather than have patients call for prescription refills, invite them to text their request. Implementing a text message option frees up your phone lines and nurses' time.

The healthcare texting tactics discussed here can also apply in other B2C scenarios, such as automobile dealerships that need to increase their service department revenue. Employing text messaging can remind customers of an oil change, tire rotation, or battery check. Accounting firms can remind clients to schedule their tax preparation. Hair and nail salons can remind customers of appointments.

Here, what works for B2C companies also can work for B2B companies. Here's just one example: Let's say you are a manufacturer who has built solid customer relationships. You enjoy face-to-face time during plant or facility visits to ensure your products or equipment is working as promised. You've already established a subscriber base to alert your customers to critical information about equipment maintenance, government regulations, or new tiered service agreements. Now, you plan to exhibit a new product at an industry tradeshow, but your customers may or may not be attending. Use text messaging marketing to encourage customers to attend the event. Invite them to your booth or presentation. Then let the handshakes—and hopefully, orders—begin.

#Fail

Cancer Research

Founded in 1953, the Cancer Research Institute (CRI) has long been a respected, well-recognized not-for-profit organization dedicated exclusively to supporting research for all cancers. However, launching a text-message campaign to raise funding for its grants and programs hit a few bumps worth noting—and avoiding. First, the SMS keyword chosen for the campaign was inexplicably changed from BEAT to DONATE. This resulted in generous donations unintentionally directed to the children's charity, UNICEF.

If that weren't bad enough, smartphone auto-correct (an annoying feature that poor typists depend on) came into play, "helping" texters with their spelling. Thanks to auto-correct, this meant that Cancer Research donors who intended to text BEAT with their pledge unwittingly texted BEAR. I'm sure these benefactors were surprised to later learn they'd symbolically adopted a polar bear via the World Wildlife Fund. Oops. The lessons here? Double- and triple-check your campaign keyword and call-to-action before the first text is launched.

Buffalo Bills

According to the Mobile Marketing Association (MMA), text message advertisers are required to disclose the number of messages subscribers can expect to receive on the advertisers' first auto-reply confirmation. Apparently, the Buffalo Bills decided that this rule didn't necessarily apply to them. The football organization was subsequently hauled off to court where they faced a hefty lawsuit for violating the TCPA. What happened to precipitate the lawsuit?

The Bills originally communicated to their subscribers that they could expect to receive three to five text messages per week for a period of 12 months. That was the promise. But after bombing subscribers with six texts the first week and seven the next, one especially aggravated subscriber filed a lawsuit. The one additional text the Bills sent the first week, and the two additional texts sent the second week cost the Bills franchise $2.5 million worth of debit cards at the team's stadium or online store, and more than half a million dollars in attorney's fees. OUCH.

While some might believe lawsuits of this caliber are ridiculous and a total waste of the American judicial system, the Buffalo Bills example illustrates the importance of adhering to MMA guidelines, best practices and keeping promises.

Forget the Quotes

San Manuel Indian Bingo & Casino, located in Highland, California, advertised its text message marketing program sign-up at a Los Angeles Dodgers game. The following call-to-action displayed on the ad.

TEXT "SPRING" TO 99158.

Can you spot the problem? How many people will include the quotation marks around the word SPRING? Fact is, many people respond like robots when directed to text a keyword. I can completely understand why many Dodgers' spectators that night spent fruitless time hunting for the "quotation" marks

75

only to receive a system reply stating, "We did not understand your request." Can you say *"dazed and confused?"*

Lesson here: Never use quotation marks around your SMS keyword. Even if your SMS marketing provider accepts them, don't.

Don't Use Numbers
One advertisement that rendered me practically speechless follows. In the name of mercy, I've elected not to disclose the advertiser.

Text "NOR002" to 41411.

What? Zeroes and the letter "O." Never a good choice. How could any interested texter remember the placement of the numeral vs. the character in a confusing stream of numerals and characters. 00ps.

Text Versus Email
Email marketing is a widely accepted and popular means to attract customers to brands, businesses, websites, and potential dating matches. However, the sheer volume of spam and unwanted emails most of us receive makes recipients cringe every time they open their Inbox.

When I open my email in the morning only to be greeted with 60-plus emails delivered the night before and now waiting for my response, I become immediately stressed. Add to that more email interruptions throughout the day, leaving me drained, distracted, and despising the email inventor. But here's the interesting paradox about electronic communication: In my experience watching, talking, and working with all kinds of people, the one trigger that absolutely commands their attention is a text message. There's an immediacy to it. They stop in mid-conversation, some in mid-lovemaking, others in mid of an end-of-the-season TV finale, reach into their pocket or purse, and pull out their cell phone. *Immediacy.*

Yet, according to Chief Marketer, the web-based authority on measurable marketing, only 20% of marketers use SMS as a part of an integrated marketing strategy.

Text messaging excites. According to SinglePoint, a publically traded premier mobile marketing and payment solutions company, text messages enjoy close to a 100% open rate and most are read within the first three minutes of being sent. This is further amplified by the CTIA study that revealed an average response time of 90 minutes for an email but only 90 seconds for a text message. SMS also produces engagement rates six to eight times higher than email. With all this being said, marketers must continue to text valuable content with offers or need-to-know information to keep subscribers looking forward to the next text or risk their abdication.

Consider the following statistics:

- 33% of email addresses are dead each year due to people deleting their account, which is generally due to the large amount of SPAM (DMA) they receive
- Consumers change phone numbers—on average, 1.4 times during their lifetime, so once you have them as a subscriber and continue to provide valuable content, you can potentially have them for life

- The average individual checks their phone approximately 150 times per day (Nokia)
- 20% of opt-in emails are opened (Frost & Sullivan / Slicktext)
- 29% of tweets are read (Frost & Sullivan / Slicktext)
- 16% of Facebook posts are read (Facebook/comScore)
- SMS campaigns experience seven times greater performance than email campaigns (Moto Message)
- SMS messages have a 19% click-through rate (cellIt)
- Emails have a 4.2% click-through rate (Anchor Mobile)
- 98% of text messages are read (Frost & Sullivan / Slicktext)

What do these statistics tell us? First, that text message marketing beats the foo out of email marketing in terms of awareness and absorption. Second, it's not harnessed nearly enough by B2C or B2C marketers. Third, text message marketing is widely overlooked as a part of an integrated marketing strategy—and customer touch point—offering tremendous opportunities for businesses to gain customer loyalty. Customer loyalty equates to increased sales and potential new customers who are referred to your business through offer- or informational-sharing.

Let's look at some of the statistics above. SMS has eight times the response rate of email marketing. 90% of SMS users read their messages within the first three minutes of receiving them. If you want to drive real-time response or take immediate action to boost sales during a particularly slow day, SMS is the more effective means.

Finally, let's talk proximity. Chances are, your customers have their mobile phones within an arm's length. The same can't be said about email, whether they receive emails at home or at work. Sure, they can check their email from a smartphone but the emails they receive don't trigger an immediate alert. Again, *immediacy*.

But text has its shortcomings too, which is why it should remain *a part* of an integrated marketing strategy and not the exclusive tactic. Here's why: Text is limited by its own nature to 160 characters, which means it cannot describe the who, what, where, when, why and how that an email can. Second, text does nothing to build brand image from a visual standpoint. Third, while it's possible to link to web pages, this only applies to web-enabled phones. At the end of the day, smart marketing is about blending the right mix. Each media has its advantages (and disadvantages). It's up to you to develop your own mix using the information and tools that offer the best hope of gain.

Next-Gen Messaging Apps: Will it Kill SMS Marketing?

Next-gen messaging apps began as "over-the-top" applications to avoid texting charges. These apps have since grown into an exciting social media portal that is taking users' attention from Facebook and Twitter. Apps like WhatsApp use far less data than social networking sites and avoids the cost of text messages.

A few years ago BlackBerry Messenger (BBM) service and the iMessage by Apple introduced the next generation of messaging apps. Marketers and analysts began speculating what this could mean to the world of mobile and if these apps would supplant SMS. They were gravely mistaken. These particular apps limited use to the OS platform, so iOS users (iPhones, iPads and iPods) could only talk to each other. Given that Android phones outnumber iOS, you can certainly see the error in the speculation.

WhatsApp received a lot of air play when Facebook purchased the company for a rumored $19 billion. While WhatsApp touts a claim of more than 450 million users worldwide, SMS subscribers number 5 billion-plus. That number is continuing to grow, by the way, not diminish.

Whose numbers are diminishing? Who's being affected by the popularity of apps like Snapchat, Kik, Tango, Line and WeChat? Facebook and Twitter. These are the companies that have to be fearful of new messaging apps. Teens are the largest majority using "over-the-top" (OTT) messaging platforms. Next-gen messaging apps are fun, shiny, "free," new ways to communicate compared to simple text messaging. This is another reason behind Facebook's purchase of WhatsApp. However, when teens really want to communicate with a business, they still use SMS.

While large brands are marketing on these apps, they're just getting their toes wet. McDonalds, Dunkin Donuts, Pepsi and Taco Bell have used some of these apps in their marketing campaigns but the apps have a smaller user base, few analytics and are still green compared to text message marketing. It's going to take some time before any of these will grow to be a major player in the mobile marketing strategy.

These next-gen messaging apps are quite appealing, both from a cost perspective and aesthetics. It is ridiculous to think of

Verizon charging $0.20/text to customers who don't sign up for a messaging plan over an infrastructure that already exists thanks to voice calls. It occupies a minuscule amount of bandwidth on their airwaves leaving the carriers to bank huge profits. Analysts' estimates put global SMS revenue around $100 billion/year. However, I don't see the major carriers changing their non-plan texting pricing policy anytime soon.

Let's look at the economics from the consumer side of things. If a brand sends out 5,000 messages via WhatsApp, they would pay around a penny in data fees based on a $25 cost for a two-gigabyte data plan. At a non-plan rate of $0.20/message, the recipient of the message would be out about $1,000. Of course, this would require the subscriber to have a smartphone to take advantage of the WhatsApp option.

The growth of OTT apps is inevitable. Expect carriers to start restructuring their pricing plans to make SMS more enticing for people to continue to use. We're starting to see this already. Also, watch for carriers to provide their own peer-to-peer, instant messaging apps. They already have the advantage of a large subscriber base to make their success attainable if done right.

Summary

Too many companies start backwards when it comes to mobile marketing. They start with tactics, like I need an app, or augmented reality. Sure they have a great cool factor. Unfortunately, they don't align the technology with the overall marketing strategy. You have to start with the goals in mind and figure out what components will get you to the goals and which are mission critical.

People ask me all the time where to start their mobile marketing strategy. If they don't tell me much about their overall goals and marketing strategy, I tell them two places. First, a mobile-friendly website. Second, text message marketing. One of many reasons that websites come first is because that opens up more ways to utilize the texts that are sent. Text is extremely important because only 65% of mobile-carrying Americans have a smartphone and 90% of American adults have a cell phone (according to Pew Internet Project's research as of January 2014). Targeting only smartphones limits your marketing ability to speak to as many people as possible.

Text message marketing is cost-effective. Since the cost is based on the number of subscribers and/or messages you send out, the cost starts small and increases as your campaign increases in effectiveness. As you build your audience, it's the perfect avenue to communicate new mobile tactics you have implemented and drive them to the updated website or app.

Text is instantly deliverable. The average time for all mobile carriers and SMS services to send and receive a message is 7 seconds. So the longest part of the campaign is going to be coming up with the right message and entering it into the system. If you're having a bad sales day, send a text with a one-time, today-only offer. Your customers are going to get it and read it that day.

Compared to email, SMS has a high open rate. Compared to direct mail or paper coupons text messaging has a staggering usage rate according to the Direct Marketing Association. On many smartphones, the message comes up over the top of phone calls and apps so the user sees it immediately. There is no filtering for spam. It's permission-based so everyone who receives your text asks for it.

Text is short, simple, easy to use, permission-based and it's not an annoying phone call when we really don't' want to talk on the phone anymore.

Even though texting has become ubiquitous across all demographics, SMS marketing has not received overwhelming acceptance and adoption by businesses. Mail costs continue to rise. Our inboxes continue to be abused by an onslaught of digital mail. It should be the time to find a marketing channel that people want, that people sign up to use, that people ask for.

Although text messaging is not the right choice for every customer, it can turn out to be the best medium for your target customers. You know the ones that love your brand, the ones that want to hear from you. While you may try to communicate through direct mail, email or billboards, are you really reaching them at the time they want to hear from you or with the message they want to hear? Drive engagement with your best customers and they will be loyal to you.

The era of shotgun marketing has gone the way of the dinosaur. Customers today want targeted, personalized messages on the most intimate device they own—their mobile phone. Exclusive, timely and unique messages create a bond that cements the relationship. Text messaging can help create that.

Now is the time to develop trust by determining the optimal message and timing. Now is the time to deliver personalized messaging to your customers. By-pass slow development processes, side-step long marketing channels and leverage the power of engagement through text message marketing today.

Epilogue

Just so you know that text messages aren't simply marketing tools only, I had to include a few of my favorite "unique" texting examples.

Holy Cow

Bessie, are you ready? (wink, wink, nudge, nudge)
Swiss professors and farmers have teamed up to solve a problem. What problem? Due to the growing demand of milk production on dairy cows, they are showing fewer signs of being in heat. Swiss farmers are finding it more difficult to determine via visual inspection when it's time to bring the bull in. A sensor is implanted into the cows and a device is affixed to the cow's neck that detects motion. The results are combined and if the cow is in heat, the device sends an SMS to the farmer. The recognition rate? About 90%. While the estimated cost is about $1,400, missing the right moment can cost the farmer $320 for each unused semen.

Don't have a cow, dude.
Although smartphones maybe standard for urban businesses, the rural farmer doesn't share the need, desire or financing. They are generally relegated to feature phones and, often, don't have access to Internet connectivity anyway. This in mind, Su

Kahumba (Green Dreams TECH Ltd), a Kenyan farmer, developed a subscription service where

- People are alerted to vital days of cows' gestation periods
- Helps farmers find the nearest vet and AI providers
- Collects and stores farmer milk and breeding records
- Sends farmers dairy prices
- Optimizes nutrition and calf care
- Can track each cow individually

Example: Send the following SMS messages to 5024 (Safaricom, Airtel and Orange), each SMS costs Ksh 5/-

- To find a vet follow the example: Vet#county#location#
  e.g vet#nakuru#njoro#
- To register a cow by birth date: Birth#cowname#date of birth#
  e.g birth#maria#2007-08-19#

The dairy industry in Kenya is a Kshs 40 billion industry based on 1.6 million farmers. Most of the farmers are bound to rudimentary methods and unable to have access that some easily afford or have access to. To stay above the poverty line, they must sell 15 liters a day yet most smallholder farmers sell 3-5 times less than that. This is a way to help maximize their production.

Who's afraid of the big bad wolf?

Sheep! Owners come in at a close second. The Swiss, already active in bovine reproduction, have been experimenting with sheep too. The sheep are fitted with a heart monitor. When the change in the heartbeat is significant enough, a wolf-repellent is released and a text message is sent to the shepherd. The device is targeted at owners who don't have enough money for a good sheep dog or in tourist areas where guard dogs are not appropriate.

Who You Gonna Call? Forget Calling, Text the Dallas Police Department

The Dallas Area Rapid Transit Police Department launched a program where people can use their cell phones to alert police to suspicious activity. Using the short-code 41411 and the keyword DARTpolice, people can anonymously text any non-emergency situations for the police to investigate. The cell numbers do not accompany the information sent so people can freely text in confidence.

Translate this to your business. Give your employees the opportunity to anonymously alert HR as to any wrong-doings. They may not want to be associated with the infraction in fear of repercussions to their career. This may range from sexual harassment to theft by managers that could fire them or make their lives intolerable. Give employees the opportunity to vote on employee of the month or highlight employees for their good work. Allow them to send ideas in that could make the workplace better. Give customers the opening to alert you to customer service issues or the need to clean the bathrooms without worrying about being put on a mailing list.

And one that I would love to see the US get to...

SMS & Taxes

This is not a new thing. In 2004, Norwegians were able to file their tax return via SMs. Closer to home, Illinois is making progress in relation to the tax process. In an effort to avoid calls and emails related to tax refunds and alleviating the pain of taxpayers continuously checking their bank account or inboxes, they can now sign up for a texting service that alerts them to the status of their tax refunds.

While the EZ tax forms could certainly be done in the States, I'm not sure we'll see it anytime soon. However, I do expect to see more states and even the federal government add text services to their process. The ability to send messages when the taxes have been received, process and fund delivered would be a welcome change and improve the experience dramatically.

About the Author

Judd Wheeler's history includes such titles as Director of Interactive Multimedia, Director of Sales and Marketing, Owner & Founder. At the root of everything resides a technology strategist, a future analyst, a trend seeker and a fad buster. He has worked in both the B2B and B2C world with clients ranging from startups to Fortune 500 clients like Merck, 3M, Koch Industries, Bayer and CITGO.

Staying at the edge of marketing technologies, he led the creation of multimedia, Internet, digital signage, DVD development and social media departments. He delivered breakthrough software solutions for businesses that increased revenue, decreased costs and improved employee engagement while creating additional mobile solutions to revolutionize the way businesses operate.

Judd fortunes include travelling overseas to speak giving him the opportunity to learn how people use mobile technology across the globe. While his work has won numerous awards over the years, his biggest awards come from conversations with business owners and marketers who have benefitted from his insight.

Judd produced the first mobile conference of its kind in his region and co-founded a group designed to bring marketers, entrepreneurs, mobile developers and the curious together to nurture and grow the mobile focus of his community. He continues to benefit from working mobile experts that continually amaze him with their innovation and desire to further mobile technology.

Get more mobile marketing tips on his blog:
www.themobilists.com

Connect with the author

Twitter: https://twitter.com/juddwheeler

LinkedIn: https://www.linkedin.com/in/juddwheeler

www.ingramcontent.com/pod-product-compliance
Lightning Source LLC
Chambersburg PA
CBHW071751170526
45167CB00003B/996